Dr. Jackson Speaks

KINGDOM QUEST

(A Trio of Revelation on the Pursuit of Victorious Living)

"I AM" Fellowship Ministries

DR. CECILIA JACKSON

authorHOUSE®

AuthorHouse™
1663 Liberty Drive
Bloomington, IN 47403
www.authorhouse.com
Phone: 1 (800) 839-8640

Published by AuthorHouse 09/27/2017

ISBN: 978 1 5462-0934-8 (sc)
ISBN: 978 1 5462-0962-1 (e)

Print information available on the last page.

This book is printed on acid-free paper.

Scripture taken from The Holy Bible, King James Version. Public Domain

THE TRIO

DO NOT FEED THE BEARS
(Victory Over Depression, Resentment, and Anger)

IT'S IN THE HEM OF HIS GARMENT
*(God's Prescription: Receiving Emotional
and Physical Healing)*

FROM PRESS TO PASSION
(The Creature is Grumbling)
(Adjusting Your View of Kingdom Advancement)

Acknowledgments

I appreciate you Dr. Michael Jackson, my wonderful husband. Your encouragement and unfailing love have energized me to continue writing. My three adult children, many thanks for the times you all have told me to keep writing in spite of obstacles, and have given me reasons to smile. As I pray for you, I know you will fulfill your destiny in Christ. To my many family members, friends, and ministry associates; this work would not have materialized without your continued words of love and support. Your prayers have helped to uphold me. Thank you.

Preface

A quest is a search, a journey, a pursuit, or a chase after something. A quest for understanding and perfecting one's life in the Kingdom of God is a noble odyssey. The book *Kingdom Quest (A Trio of Revelation on the Pursuit of Victorious Living)* guides and counsels the reader in **overcoming challenges** with: depression, anger, resentment, bitterness, emotional and physical depletion, and a mindset of mediocrity regarding life in general. The reader's thinking is propelled with **fresh discoveries and approaches** to **mending goals, recovering passion for living**, and **gaining wholeness** and healing for one's entire being!! The book *Kingdom Quest* includes a trio of books within a book that target problem trends in the lives of individuals; furthermore, each section generates renewed insight and inspires suggested strategies that help solve problems and foster Kingdom dominion.

Table of Contents

DO NOT FEED THE BEARS
(Victory Over Depression, Resentment, and Anger)

IT'S IN THE HEM OF HIS GARMENT
(God's Prescription: Receiving Emotional and Physical Healing)

FROM PRESS TO PASSION and
The Creature is Grumbling
(Adjusting Your View of Kingdom Advancement)

DO NOT FEED THE BEARS

(Victory Over Depression, Resentment, and Anger)

Introduction

There are areas in every Christian's life that present challenges. These areas are usually the places where we are weakest. Of course, the desire of the adversary is to cause us to get weaker and weaker even to the point of allowing our challenges to overtake us. God has already shown us in his word ways we can become victorious over every challenge.

Some of the areas Christians are often challenged in are: coping with depression, resentment, and anger. This reading shares simple Biblical help with what I have chosen to call "Bears". The allegorical thought of these challenge areas being "bears" we face, comes from my family's many visits to the mountains where one often reads literature about the hazards of feeding the bears and other helpful pointers for camping outdoors. Also, I've gleaned from the rare times when we have seen (close enough) real "bears"! It is not a bright idea to feed these large lurking, hungry creatures. To do so will cause a person and their friends and loved ones to be hurt, and it could be fatal. This is true with the "bears" of depression, resentment and anger. This section of the first trio of the book Kingdom Quest shares in a brief, yet powerful manner, how to walk in victory over these challenges.

CHAPTER ONE

Depression – A Sunken Place

D o you sometimes feel you are so despondent that you do not want to get up in the morning? Are you often in a mental state wherein you can only cry, cry, and keep crying? Do you often withdraw from others, feel sorry for yourself, feel suicidal, extremely angry, eat and eat yet the hunger is not satisfied? Do you go periods of time without eating, but you are predisposed with thinking about failures and disappointments or times when you were happy in the past? What's wrong with you? You are depressed.

To be depressed means you are in a sunken place where your spirit is sad. You are extremely discouraged which has caused a reduction in the quality of life God has intended you to have. Not only is your vitality low, but your very will to fight can be challenged.

There are many things that can cause one to land in this condition of depression. Doctors have published recent study showing the medical and biological effects of light on human beings. Thus, Seasonal Affective Disorder (SAD) is said to be depressive episodes based on seasonal variations and exposure to light. Certain people are sensitive in the winter where there is less exposure to sunlight. Giving them excessive artificial light is supposed to help lift them from their "sunken place".

Menopause with its accompanying hormonal imbalances can cause depression is some women. Often restoring the proper hormones to nature's balance will relieve or eliminate depression in such cases.

Physical problems can cause depression, such as surgery; or even the news of physical problems can cause one to sink to a low place in their emotions. There are also common experiences such as: loss of a loved one, loss of employment and financial stress, feelings of not accomplishing goals or dreams, and the list goes on and on. All of these experiences are painful, especially when they linger to months and even years.

These types of depression are *bears* we as Christians and non-Christians sometimes face. Yet, even though their presence is not wanted and often they come upon you by surprise, you cannot waddle in the circumstances and let them keep you pressed down in a sunken place. To do so is like feeding these *bears* and the end result is they will come into your very home (your heart, your life) and destroy you.

They won't stop there. They will affect the people you love most. Bears don't just choose to attack adults. Children are not a restricted area from these troubles. If you do not choose to fight them off with the proper tools that will send them running from you, they will hang around until they not only destroy you, but your children, wife, husband, and friends too are all fair game. When you are depressed, your mental and emotional state has an impact upon others close in your community of support.

Although there may be some difficult challenges Christians face, you must above all, remember that God's word says he has made a way of escape for you that you may stand in spite of the difficulties (I Cor. 10:13). There is a way of escape! There is a winning posture you can assume for any challenge that you are faced with. The Holy Spirit has given you power to rise from any sunken place to an elevated place of victory!

CHAPTER TWO

Expectations and a New Attitude

I have found that one of the most effective ways to move from a state of depression is to develop a new attitude about the circumstances you are faced with and to set reasonable expectations or goals for your life. Too many unrealistic goals can cause depression.

Short-term and long-term goals must be set for one's life. If all you have set are goals that will take a long time to accomplish, you won't have any short victories to celebrate. You won't even realize that you are making progress toward those long-term goals because you won't be able to see the final result until later on down the road of life. Therefore, you can get depressed and feel sunken even though progress is being made.

Set short-term goals so you can see God doing wonders for you on a daily and weekly basis. Celebrate those accomplishments! This will set you on a new course of having a new attitude about your life. It is imperative that you develop the attitude that God is good and that he is working ALL things out in your life for your good. Your attitude shapes your outcome!

Many people set unrealistic expectations and become depressed and angry with God when their goals and expectations aren't met. Set realistic expectations. If you know it took you five years to gain an excess of seventy pounds over weight, don't expect it to take five days to lose the weight. If you were born with brown eyes, you will more than likely have brown eyes until Jesus returns. Don't pray for blue eyes and get disappointed when your eye color does not change. Buy yourself some blue contact lenses and be happy. If it takes four years of college to qualify for the kind of job you desire, stop *claiming* the job position you don't qualify for, believing it will be given to you (calling this faith). Instead, go to the business office of the college of your choice and fill out financial support applications and scholarship applications to get the money to attend college to qualify for the *dream* job you want God to give you. This would be God's kind of faith. Next, go to school and study. Then graduate from school and go get the job. Chart your time frame for this long-term goal and celebrate God meeting your needs in other positions of employment until your final desire comes to pass. Rejoice as you accomplish each short-term goal that leads to your long-time goal. Set realistic goals and walk toward them both practically and spiritually. Keep in mind that you are a spiritual being, but you live in a physical body and must adjust your mind to think by the dictates of God's word and by doing so, order your body according.

Be realistic. If the father of your children is not financially supporting his children and you are financially depleted trying to care for them, pray for God to change his heart and to save him and yes, walk by faith to believe his heart will change; however, in the mean time until the prayer is answered don't let depression, SAD, or allow disappointment to keep you in a sunken place. Go to the legal authorities and process whatever paper work that needs to be processed legally in order to get the support that is due you to help care for your children! God is not getting any glory in your children suffering and you smiling on the outside, while frustrated, depressed, and torn up on the inside because your "X" is taking good care of his new lady and her children, yet neglecting his responsibility for your children. Get out of that sunken place and set some realistic expectations and God will meet you in the process of walking forward with your plans!

CHAPTER THREE

Think Optimistically

I am convinced that circumstances are sometimes not as bad as they seem once we deal with the reality of reasonable expectations and develop new attitudes about our situations. However, even when things are genuinely difficult, you need to learn how to cultivate habits of positive thinking. This is merely thinking in a manner that scripture dictates. Paul told the saints at the church in Philippi to think on the things that were true and lovely and just and pure (Philippians 4:8). He said that if anything is worthy of praise or worthy to brag about, anything worthy of giving time to in one's thoughts, then it should be those things that are good. That is still the word of God to you today. Don't spend time thinking about sadness or pain; it will only keep you depressed. That's just feeding the bear of depression. Think good, happy, wholesome, winning thoughts!

So, what does one do while going through difficult circumstances? Even in the middle of these bear-like experiences, find something to be thankful for. Be positive. Look for and point out something good, something you can be glad about while undergoing a hard time. Positive reflections contribute to changed attitudes and raised mental altitudes about succeeding in life. Often you are not capable of changing your heart, but if you continually ask the Holy Spirit to do the work of transforming your mind, you can keep growing and thriving while triumphing over what could potentially cut off all life in you. The Spirit of the Lord will change your heart when you obey the word of God and move forward with mind transformation which conditions your mind to think His way during your times of challenge.

Paul and Silas exercised the secret of being thankful and thinking optimistically in all things. When they were thrown in prison in Philippi, beaten and put into stocks, at midnight they began to sing praises to God. Even the other prisoners began to listen to their new songs created in the middle of their circumstance (Acts 16: 11–40). The end result was good. They were eventually set free. This was the result of their optimistic attitude while they were going through something awful. These were ordinary men, no different from you or me. What could happen if you started to sing and praise God through what you are going through! God would set you free from it.

I went through an illness one summer that really set me back, so I thought. It was during a time that I was working on the completion of my Masters of Education degree at Xavier University. The ministry was growing and moving and I was right in the center of some very exciting things when a physical attack came upon me which restricted me to being home, with the inability to move my body to even go to the restroom without my husband's assistance. I had never felt pain in such magnitudes. The greatest pain was when we took the children to the train station to meet my oldest son as he was coming home that summer from college and I would have greeted him in a wheelchair. People who knew me knew that I was not one to be immobile. The physicians had diagnosed me with inflammation of the brain and symptoms of what appeared to be a mild stroke. When I heard these words I felt myself sinking to a low place. I cried each time my husband had to help me from the sofa to the restroom. I had taken enough medicines to lose track of how often I was taking this pill or that, yet nothing seemed to give me relief unless I was in such a deep sleep that I felt in a state between consciousness and unconsciousness.

I did not have the strength to sing aloud, but I began to sing softly to myself and to sing to my spirit new songs of praise to God and prayers for God's supernatural touch. It was time to be optimistic. I had already told my husband not to tell the details of my condition to the church family or to some of my family. It was not a matter of pride, but an issue of not wanting to alarm others and not wanting anyone feeling sorry for me. Also, I did not want to begin feeling sorry for myself. I listened to the word of

God recorded, prayed, and praised my heart into a positive attitude. My proclamation was, "I will live and not die, in order to declare the works of the Lord, which is my purpose." I found a way to be thankful during a time of much pain and disappointment. I declared that God had his own way of allowing me time with him to get to know him better. I declared it to be a season of rest for me, no matter what medical science and medical terminology called it. I went on a journey with the Lord that led me to total healing. The result was when I greeted my son, he saw me standing! When I returned to the house of the Lord, I returned with strength and joy! Part of what I had to do was, think myself happy (Acts 26:2), believe against what *appeared* to be fact and stand on what *was* fact; because of his stripes I am healed (Is. 53:5)!

I was in school when the attack came, so God moved on the hearts of men and gave me favor! The university accepted my doctor's reports and worked with me to do independent studies in order to graduate on time! My job awarded me the sick time needed to start work two months later that fall! All was well. I learned from Paul and Silas to order and command the atmosphere in what *seemed* to be *my* prison, so that freedom would come. Freedom and healing came!

An optimistic view in the center of what may seem to be an eye of a storm causes one to think, act, and react according to scripture. You can rehearse the word of Paul when he said we are afflicted in many ways, but we are not crushed. Sometimes we are puzzled, but we are not driven to despair. We are persecuted, but not forsaken. Sometimes we are struck down, but we are not destroyed. We always have memory of the death of Jesus so that the life of Jesus will be made visible in our bodies (2 Corinthians 4:8-10)! You are alive and create life when we think optimistically!

CHAPTER FOUR

Don't Feed the Bears of Resentment and Hurt

Your honest emotional responses to the following questions and statements will help you to determine if you are possibly harboring resentment in your heart. Have you lost your job and there are others whom you feel should have been downsized rather than you? Do you feel upset because you never seem to have the money for the things you need, but it bothers you that others who seem not as *righteous* as you, are prospering? Does this make you angry? Did a religious leader disappoint you and you'd prefer to never be around them, or most other believers and churches as well? Do you always seem to be at the right place at the wrong time in order to get the opportunities you deserve? Does your health, ethnic classification, education, or appearance seem to prevent you from getting a break in life? Did your children, wife, husband, friend, or relative hurt you and cause you to avoid establishing relationships with others? Do you frequently use these words, "I won't forget that"? After responding to these questions think about the meaning of the word *resentment*; which means to hold a grudge against someone, to be annoyed with individuals because of an insult or disagreement, or to hold deep-seated ill will against another person. After this personal inventory and looking at the definition of *resentment*, you should now have an idea (for certain) if you are carrying resentment.

If you are not feeding the bear of resentment, skip this chapter and read on. If you are feeding this hungry creature that wants to live in your heart, then read this chapter prayerfully and allow the Spirit of the Living God to touch your heart and change you. If your answer was yes to the survey questions – you should read this chapter. Reading this chapter can also help you to encourage and counsel others in your relationship circle who may be embracing resentment.

Holding on to grudges and resentment takes a concentrated effort. You have to utilize a large amount of energy to nurse a grudge, and to remember why you are so angry and upset, especially after time passes. Individuals who have resentment also attempt to persuade others and to justify the magnitude of their ill will. You will rekindle the flame of passion for the grudge if it begins to wane. If you continue to carry the offense long enough, it will damage you and others, even your relationship with God. Nothing anyone has ever done to you can be worth breaking your relationship with God. Let resentment go and allow the refreshing waters of the Holy Spirit to heal you. You owe this to your own self for help and healing.

For some reason, nursing a grudge can feel good at first, especially if someone has really wronged you. What happens is the feeling of self-pity is cultivated. For example you start to think: 1) After all, life isn't fair! 2) Too many opportunities have passed me by. 3) I have strong, adverse feelings because I am not as financially secure as my neighbors. 4) I feel my friends and people I trusted most have hurt me. 5) I believe I had more than my share of bad circumstances. The results, this way of thinking cultivates seeds of hurt that begin to grow into full-sized bushes or trees of resentment into your heart. What must be realized is you can hurt yourself when you hold on to grievances, pains, resentments, jealousies and the like.

Esau hated his brother Jacob because of the blessing which his father had blessed Jacob with and he felt the decision was unfair and deceitful. Esau said to himself that the days were coming close when his father would soon die and go to paradise. He thought in his heart to kill his brother Jacob. The mother, Rebekah, heard about Esau's plans and told Jacob to get out of town quickly. These brothers missed years of relationship. The Bible narrative tells of how they finally were reconciled many years later and they wept and rejoiced (Genesis 27). We learn from this story that resentment hurts us and others in relationship around us. Without a doubt, Rebekah was affected by the broken relationship of her sons, Esau and Jacob. Follow the Bible narrative to see how Rebekah, and the family handled this harbored resentment.

How can we prevent the *bears* of resentment and hurt from hanging around our cabin and coming inside to dwell? First, I'd like to suggest that you minimize your disappointment in others by recognizing that no one is perfect. You are not perfect. It is inevitable that people will hurt you. Some will hurt you intentionally and set out to cause trouble for you. Others will not mean you any harm, but their actions or lack of response will hurt you. Whenever you are involved in friendships and relationships with others, you automatically set yourself up for hurt and disappointment. Yet, at the same time, you set yourself up for happiness. That is just the way it works with humans. Hurt is inevitable; it's what you do with the hurt that determines your success in life. Release it; don't embrace it.

So realize that no one is perfect and love them for how God has made them in spite of their weaknesses and the way they sometimes behave. Minimize your disappointment in the behavior of others by remembering that no one is perfect. Not even you. Consider that if the individual is a believer who is determined to develop into a mature, Christian; then God is still working on them as he is still working on you.

Jesus knew mankind would error when working together, simply because of human nature. Some say love your neighbors and hate your enemy, but God's command is to love your enemies and pray for those who do you harm so that we can all develop as sons of our heavenly Father. He causes the sun to rise and set on the evil and the good individuals and sends rain on both (Matt. 5:45).

He says if you love only those who love you, the reward is small because it is easy to do this and even non-believers can successfully practice this law. So, if you practice this behavior then you as Christians are no better than non-believers and your mind has not been renewed by the word of

God. A believer with a Christ-conditioned mind loves and respects both good and bad individuals.

You are to observe the higher practice which is to love those who do you wrong (Matthew 5). You can learn to love people for who they are, only if you look to God for your reward. You cannot depend on others and their approval. You are free from the bondage of human expectation as you look to God for his love and approval.

Grudges are released if you first do not allow them an opportunity to lodge in your heart. Second, if you expect others to error and remember they are not perfect beings, then you will not become so disappointed when others make mistakes and hence hold resentment against them as associated with their errors. This frees you from taking on the bear of resentment.

Furthermore, you can avoid feeding resentment and hurt by allowing the healing waters of forgiveness to flow through your life even when others do not. This is a personal choice. Grudges can be eliminated if you keep hurt from becoming full-blown by quickly forgiving the person who has hurt us. I really mean, quickly forgiving the person. We must be immediate with our forgiveness, whether we are the offended party or the one who offended someone else. Sincerely apologize and make restitution immediately. This enables you to move on and not become bitter. It keeps the heavens open to your prayers and causes your praise to be heard by God, and your relationship with him pure.

The apostle Peter called Jesus his closest friend. He walked and talked with the Lord for three years. He understood the mission of Christ clearly, possibly more than others as we consider some of his responsibilities in scripture. In spite of this, Peter denied his Lord three times, not once or twice. He repeated his weakness. Jesus responded by asking Peter to make a recommitment of his love. Then he allowed Peter to repent and begin again with no soiled past (John 21). This is a fine example of forgiveness and a decision to not allow resentment to rule because Peter's denials could have cost Jesus his very life.

We find another fine example in the life of Paul. God gave him another opportunity after failure. Paul had been a murderer and a zealot, yet God extended to him a new life. This was contrary to the feelings of the leaders in the early church. They were not eager to give (Paul) Saul a second opportunity because they were afraid of him since his past actions were brutal demonstrations towards Christians. Barnabas received Saul and was willing to give him the benefit of the doubt. Barnabas was willing to risk his life for Saul, believing he had truly changed. That kind of action established the way, and set an example for Christians today.

The young nephew of Paul, John Mark, wanted the excitement of going on a missionary journey; but soon after he left Paul and Barnabas, for some reason, John Mark decided that he did not want to continue, so he left and went back to Jerusalem (Acts 13).

Later, when Paul wanted to return to the churches they had previously ministered to in order to check up on the believers there, Barnabas suggested they include John Mark, but Paul disagreed. He was reluctant to involve the young man again, because of the previous experience of him leaving the ministry before the mission was complete. They decided to separate into two groups: Barnabas took John Mark and sailed to Cyprus and Paul and Silas went to Syria and Cilicia (Acts 15). Later in Paul's ministry, he mentions John Mark as being a very useful servant (2 Timothy 4:11).

We need more Barnabas-like spirits today – those who will extend to others a second chance. We also need more people with the spirit of Paul. He was willing to forgive and forget John Mark's past and his weaknesses and activated his forgiveness by spreading a good reputation about his brother Mark's going forward with Barnabas in ministry; when he could have spread destructive information at the time of separation.

Reflect on these situations relative to today's Christians. Believers seem eager to tear one another down at times, rather than build one another up in Christ. This has frequently happened at times of separation regarding different views about how to implement ministry.

Individuals have been called *cursed, sheep thieves,* and other degrading names. In some extreme cases leaders have forbidden their members from associating with other members of the body of Christ completely. Such actions are certainly motivated by the *accuser* of the body (satan) and not motivated by the love and leading of Christ. Such experiences in the Christian walk can leave bitterness and resentment if a believer is not mature enough to walk away with love and forgiveness in his or her heart.

My husband and I had a similar experience wherein we had the opportunity to make the choice of forgiving and not harboring resentment; or not forgiving and walking away with anger and bitterness in our hearts. This was a situation wherein we had labored many years in faithful support of a ministry, and extended communication and letters of support and love to the pastor and leadership team when the time came for us to relocate and to continue to fulfill our purpose in God.

Because our previous relationship had been wonderful, we made every possible effort to go forward with vision and had every expectation that good relationships would continue. We were shocked and hurt when we later learned the pastors had circulated harmful, degrading, inflammatory literature to other ministries throughout the city and to dear friends, misrepresenting our intentions and character.

The materials that were circulated were not only untrue concerning ministry intents; but they were an attack on our personal character, which had taken years of consistent living to build. Of course this was not a pleasurable feeling, especially when these persons were those whom we had placed ultimate confidence in, had built long term relationships with, and had served and protected in ministry with all our hearts for many years. What does one do? Make mature and liberating choices. Realize all human beings are subject to error. Choose to forgive the parties involved, refuse to hold resentment in your heart, and leave it to the Lord to take care of the rest. Also, walk in close relationship with other strong believers and leaders who can support you in receiving your healing, rather than cuddling the hurt and making it your friend.

You may say, "That is not an easy thing to do". I tell you from experience this was not an easy thing to do, but it became easier and easier as we were determined we would obey God's prescription for healing and walking forward in peace, joy, and the spirit of forgiveness.

We all learn and grow through the things we suffer. In addition, we learn in the fire or crucible of events just what our own character is made of. My husband and I received many calls from others who knew us well, and had worked with us for years in ministry. They were appalled at the situation. We refused to entertain even that communication as support; but instead, asked them to pray for all involved because "Godly sorrow works repentance to salvation."(II Cor. 7:10).

Others we worked with in the secular field heard about the matter, saw copies of the documents written, and were incensed. They were encouraging us to take legal action and were agreeing to help with financial support to do so. We had paperwork and written documentation that could have supported this idea to win the case, but we had to ask ourselves who would win in the end. We could have walked away with finances from legal action for being slandered, but that would not have appeased the hurt from the destructive arrow of Christian brothers. Only the Holy Spirit could have really won in this case and that was if we allowed him to get in, and stay in the arena in the center of the crucible -- and that is what we chose to do. We surrounded ourselves with believers who not only interceded for us, but also encouraged our little ones who, of course, were affected by the situation. We were determined to be better and not bitter from the matter, and God met us in the middle of the mess! He made a mess into a miracle!

On occasions we were at services and prophets called us out and described how the enemy had used people we loved to throw fiery darts at us and a stone that would have destroyed us, but the angels of the Lord stood between the destroyer and us and delivered us. One prophet stated that the arrows were sent to pierce, but He/God had reversed them and was using them to point the way to greener pastures where he had already ordained for us new relationships on the foundation of God's love and his word.

Our hearts rejoiced, especially since God had sent the word of prophecy to us from vessels of whom we had never met nor even seen in our lives! We needed those words of love, direction, and support from God to assure us that we could walk through that storm and that the word we had been taught (even by these same leaders) was indeed true! Because of our obedience, not only did the Lord bless, heal, keep, and revive us – but he used this trial for our good and thrust us forward into new fruitful revelations and relationships! Above that, he blessed and anointed our seed!

Why did God move for us? Because we took the first step and moved toward God by choosing to follow the Scripture's pattern during the fire of the trial. We refused to feed the bears of resentment, hurt, and anger. Instead, we chose to walk in forgiveness. The Bible states that if we forgive men, our heavenly father will forgive us, but if we do not forgive our brothers and sisters neither will God the father forgive and remember us. We refused to nurse the pain, but allowed the Lord to heal it. We refused to shut off those who acted ungodly, but chose to forgive them. These were still our brothers and sisters in the Lord.

The end result is we still visit the congregation today when we choose too. The Lord has restored the relationships and we thank him because his word is true. The results of our faith and obedience have rewarded us with God's favor. Furthermore, God is using this experience to also minister hope and life to others who are going through hurts from Christians in the Church. Just as God had those who were like Barnabas to us, we are now like Barnabas to others. If you choose to be better and not bitter, God will use your life to bless others. It will be a testimony of the power of God that is able to heal, deliver, forgive, and teach you the love and compassion of God.

A final way to keep resentment and hurt from building up is to minimize your own disappointment with God. Follow me on this one. It seems a strange bit of advice, but it's important. Often we set ourselves up for disappointment in God because we tell God how to answer our prayers and how to run our lives. We give him great details; we become presumptuous in our expectations of his honoring our requests, often not consulting him for his plan for any of the episodes of our life. Then, when our prayers are not answered the way we thought best, or the way we told him to answer, then we feel God has failed us or let us down. Our faith begins to weaken, we wonder if God really cares, and the seeds of resentment are sown and begin to grow seeds against the love and faithfulness of God toward us.

Remember the prayer in Matthew chapter six requests the kingdom of God to come and His will to be done on earth as it is done in heaven. Although it is scriptural to pray for the desires of your hearts to be met, what about praying for the will of God for your life more often than praying for your desires? I have found that this works to minimize disappointment and makes you more receptive to what God is doing and wants to do in your life. By praying this way, you pray for the will of God to be done in your life first, and that he orders your steps so that your will lines up with His will. In his will there is no disappointment because it is the path that pleases him, thus it launches an arrow of peace and joy that goes straight to the heart giving you freedom from hurts and resentment. There is no peace comparable to resting in the bosom of His purpose, His destiny for your life. Resentment and hurt are bears you cannot afford to befriend.

CHAPTER FIVE

Anger Can be a Bear

Anger is a feeling of antagonism and displeasure usually resulting from opposition or conflict. Anger is a sign that you are alive and well whereas hate is a sign that one is sick and needs to be healed. Healthy anger can drive you to do something to change situations in your life that may need to be changed. It can energize you to make things better. You are allowed to be angry, but when angry you must not sin (Psalms 4:4). Anger can be a positive force or a negative energy.

One way to get rid of the negative energy of anger is to simply forgive. In other words you can get angry about a matter, but immediately work on forgiving the person for whatever was done to make you angry. Sometimes when your mind says you have forgiven a person who wronged you, you may feel you have not forgiven because your emotions still remember the anger at the time the event occurred.

Memory is part of your brain function. It is a God-given ability. Some things are stored in the short-term memory and others are stored in the long-term memory. The term of *memory* usually depends upon how often something is rehearsed. That something can be a math lesson, a memory scripture, or an offense. That's why it is important to avoid rehearsing hurt and anger and any negative occurrences, because it will become a part of the long-term memory and thus harder to forget. This increases the risk of you becoming bitter and holding resentment. When you are quick to forgive, then the pain, or offense lies only in the short-term memory;

thus the incident is more quickly forgotten. Yet, because the mind can remember the offense, does not mean it hasn't been forgiven. It takes time to forget. Your intricate web of memories is not like a slate that you can just wipe clean. So, although you can remember an incident, you could very well have already begun the process of consciously forgiving the person associated with the experience. So, you can walk in forgiveness and still have memory of a situation.

Forgiveness offers you a way to minimize the pain associated with the ill done and the opportunity to go on with your life. As you go on with life, time will cause the memory to fade away. You can see persons who have wronged you in a new light of compassion not necessarily justifying their acts toward you, but releasing both them and yourself from the negative situation and negative energy of anger. This moves you toward total healing and reconciliation.

When you start to understand forgiveness the way scripture requires you to live, passages in the scripture become clearer to you. Ephesians chapter four says to not let the sun go down while you are angry. This lets you know that conflict may not be solved before the sun goes down; however, you are to forgive quickly – before the sun goes down (before you go to bed). You are not to lie down at the end of any day with anger in your heart. You can operate the process of forgiveness each day. You are to practice forgiving, even as God forgave you, then you can exert every effort possible to work with the other person to completely resolve the conflict. You must understand however, that endless discussion on some issues will not ever bring them to resolve. In such cases when you have done all you can do, move forward in peace with your brother. In other words, agree to disagree and move on in love.

Peter asked Jesus how often he should forgive a fellow Christian for sinning against him. Jesus answered him saying he should forgive seventy times seven (Matthew 18: 21–22). In other words you are supposed to be willing to continually forgive each other. Obviously after forgiving someone repeatedly, you won't immediately forget what happened in succession after each incident. However, God begins to remove the pain of the encounter and as you allow God to continue to work in your life the spirit of forgiveness, you are made free. In time, as you refuse to dwell on the hurt, the angering experiences will become less memorable. Persons who continually entertain conversations about hurting incidents will slow this process of forgiveness and healing. Rather, continue to cast that concern, weight and care upon the Lord. He cares for and helps you.

One of the most difficult things to do when you are angry is to BE STILL. It is even harder to make an immediate decision to repay good for the evil done to you. This seems to be an unnatural response! Yet, that is exactly what Paul tells the church at Rome to do. He says to bless those who persecute you and do not curse them. He says to rejoice with those who rejoice and to cry with those who cry. Furthermore, he instructs the saints to live in harmony with one another avoiding haughtiness, by being lowly and never conceited. Paul instructs the church again, to repay good for evil and to live peacefully with everyone. He instructs the believers to avoid seeking vengeance because he says vengeance is the Lord's responsibility and it is certain that he will do his job. In the latter part of Romans chapter 12 God tells Paul to tell the church to feed their enemy if they are hungry and to give them water if they are thirsty; finally he says to overcome evil with good (Romans 12). This behavior enables believers to avoid feeding the bear, anger.

You can be sure that if anger is fed, a lot of other old and young bears who are friends with anger will begin to hang around your home, your heart. A few friends of anger are: hatred, resentment, bitterness, sickness, and murder. Instead of yielding to these behaviors, BE STILL and wait, and think instead of acting too hastily. Society today encourages you to defend yourself, fight back, and be aggressive. There are certainly times when you do need to be more aggressive or forward, but in the heat of anger, being cautious in the wise way of response instead of fanning the flame of fury. This causes more heartache. Practice BEING STILL, taking time to cool off.

Be careful. Do not allow anger to force you to be out-of-control. The Word of God gives some examples of persons who allowed their anger to get out of control. When Cain and Abel brought their offerings of the fruit of the ground, Cain was very angry and his countenance fell. The Lord asked him why he was so angry and why his countenance had fallen. He warned Cain that if he acted properly he would be accepted, but if he chose to lose control and remain angry, then sin was waiting at the door with the plan to control him. God wanted Cain to master sin and his own anger (Genesis 4). The end of the story reveals that Cain failed. He was so out of control that he eventually took his brother Abel out to the field and killed him. Thus, the result of his anger and loss of control was the death of his brother. Believers in our day are still killing brothers and sisters in the Lord because they are not able to control their emotions, anger and hot temper! Don't be one who causes death: death of dreams, emotional death of family relationships, psychological and spiritual death in relationships in the body of Christ because of the bear of anger. God has given us the authority to put all things under our feet, under control and this means anger as well (Eph. 1:22, Heb. 2:8).

Saul could not master his anger and it caused him to throw a spear to try to kill David. Saul's uncontrollable anger forced David to run for his life (1 Samuel 18).

Like many, you may have experienced times in your life when you have allowed your anger to get out of control. As a result, you may have embarrassed yourself, wounded others, and ruined your good Christian witness. All is not loss. Although anger can be a natural response, how you respond to the energy of anger becomes a choice and an act of your will. You can choose to respond with the mind and character of Christ, or to respond in the strength of your own will. Positive results come when you allow the Holy Spirit to control your will and by doing so, you control your anger; sometimes by walking away, giving time to cool off, just being silent, reading, listening to music, playing a sport, having a hobby, thinking about the situation, and many other successful strategies. Find what works best for you and apply it.

How can you avoid awkward, embarrassing moments resulting from displays of anger? How do you direct the energy of anger toward good?

How can you develop control over your anger? Simply obey, practice God's word:

1. Be angry, but do not sin, only commune with your hearts at night and learn to be quiet, be still (Psalms 4).
2. Give a soft answer; it will turn anger in another direction (Proverbs 15).
3. Be quick to hear others, speak less frequently and learn to listen (James 1).
4. Don't get angry so fast because anger does not reflect God's righteousness, and will result in the loss of control and even death.
5. Do not have communication or conversation with bitterness, malice, murder, and slander; but be kind, tenderhearted, and forgiving to others just as Christ forgives you (Ephesians 4).
6. Quickly forgive, even before the sun goes down and in time with the help of the Holy Spirit, you will forget.
7. Use the energy of anger to help you develop creative ways to build relationships and avoid behaviors that will entrap you in anger.
8. Allow the peace and love of God to prevail in your actions, responses and decisions.

CHAPTER SIX

Exhortation

At times many have fallen short, or given up the victory to an area of weakness. Nevertheless, it is important that you persevere to perfect Godly character. You must not feed the areas of weakness (bears) in your life, but feed your strengths. The bears of depression, resentment, and anger come to tempt you at times in your Christian walk, but God has given you power that you may triumph victoriously over them! I exhort you to use the simple instructions given in this text as practical tools of great power for an overcoming life. The scriptures in this text will strengthen you and empower you to live in victory. ***Do Not Feed the Bears!***

IT'S IN THE HEM OF HIS GARMENT

(God's Prescription: Receiving Emotional
and Physical Healing)

Introduction

God is interested in the whole person. When the word of God states that God wishes above all that we prosper and be in health even as our soul prospers, he means just that. Being in good physical health, and prosperity of the soul and spirit are necessary if we are to live effective, happy lives as Christians.

In fact, wholeness for the body, soul, and spirit are prerequisites for each of us in order to fulfill our purpose. The woman with the issue of blood whose brief story is recorded in the book of Matthew, chapter nine, is a Biblical example of someone who reached out through a crowd of circumstances and persevered to be made totally whole (healthy).

The woman in Matthew chapter nine realized there was something special for her in the garment and in the hem of the garment of Christ. It was so special that she defied the rules of man to reach the heart of God. The specific blessings she pursued were found in the echoes from her history, which provided a voice and an action of faith in her present that changed her life forever.

The contents of this section of the trio of books, *It's in the Hem of His Garment (God's Prescription: Receiving Emotional and Physical Healing)*, teaches and promotes the healing of God for the whole person as revealed through study of the woman in the Bible; Matthew, chapter nine.

CHAPTER ONE

─────── ◈ ───────

Laying the Foundation of
the Dimensions of Man

M an consists of three dimensions; body, soul, and spirit. Wholeness (completeness, health) for the **BODY** pertains to the physical realm, the outward man. Physically we feel pain. Also, all humans have basic needs: food, shelter, and love. The need for food and shelter are part of the bodily needs. The body must be cared for hygienically.

The body requires physical exercise in order for all systems to function properly. It is foolishness for a believer to neglect his or her health. The body is cared for with the use of natural things. In Christian semantics, this physical realm is called "the flesh". We should not allow the flesh to dominate, although it is an important part of the trichotomy of man. The spirit of man should control the body.

The **SOUL** is the dimension of man that deals with his intellect (intelligence, knowledge, mind) and will. It is the home of our desires and plans. It is the part of man that thinks and reasons. This includes all of one's emotions and attitudes. It is who we are: our character and personality, our tendencies both the ones that are pleasing to the Lord and the ones that displease him. This is why the word demands that we renew our mind, which is the realm of the soul. The only way that this can be done is to pray and read the word of God, which changes our distorted thinking and our rank reasoning and allows our mind to be adjusted to think like Christ thinks (the mind of Christ). Paul says we are to have the mind *transformed* (Romans 12:2).

The realm of the **SPIRIT** (Greek – pneuma) is the dimension of man that deals with spiritual insight and awareness – that God-knowing part of man. It operates the faculties of faith, hope, reverence, true love, prayer, and worship. It opens the window to communication with God again. It is the part of man that enables us to know God, to speak with him and hear him when he speaks to us.

Before the fall, in the Garden of Eden, man was in perfect *spirit* state. Remember the word of God says God walked and talked with man in the cool of the day. In other words, there was perfect relationship between God and man. When man fell or sinned in the Garden of Eden, he fell from that perfect spiritual state – that state wherein his spirit realm was one with God. The door was shut. That is why when we were unbelievers our spirits were dormant, in a sleeping state, but when we received Christ into our life, the chambers of our heart were reopened once again to the spirit of the Lord and we became **alive** and capable of direct communication with God. Then, as we followed him in water baptism allowing our old, corrupt nature to be stripped away, Paul says we rise to walk in newness of life (Romans 6:3-4). He further clarifies that a circumcision or cutting away of the old nature that occurs in water baptism is not the work of the outward expression of a Jew, but it is an inward circumcision of the heart in the SPIRIT (Colossians 2:11-12; Romans 2:28-29). Our spirit becomes **fully alive** in Christ! God is concerned about the wellness of the whole man: body, soul, and spirit!

CHAPTER TWO

Setting the Stage, the Backdrop

In the book of *Matthew,* Jesus was moving and flowing in his earthly ministry, doing demonstrations of the power given to him by the Father. To highlight a few miracles:

Chapter 4 -- *He was led by the Spirit in the wilderness to be tempted of the devil*

Chapter 5 -- *He taught the beatitudes to his disciples*

Chapter 6-- *He taught the Lord's Prayer*

Chapter 7-- *He taught the principal of receiving blessings through asking, seeking, and knocking He taught the parable of the two builders, the wise and the foolish man, one who built on sand and one who built on a rock and the rain came and the winds blew and the house on the rock was left standing*

Chapter 8 -- *Jesus healed the leper and spoke to the wind, waves, He cast devils from a man and sent the swine into the sea*

These miracles were all mentioned in a particular order and set the stage and preparation for the focus of this text, which is found in Matthew, chapter 9.

CHAPTER THREE

If I Could Touch His Garment

Read chapter nine of the book of Matthew, verses 18 – 22. While Jesus was teaching, a certain ruler came to him worshipping him saying his daughter was dead. She requested that Jesus come lay his hands upon her, afterward he believed his daughter would live. Jesus got up and followed the man and so did his disciples.

As Jesus was on the way to minister to someone else, one persistent woman caught his attention. This was a WOMAN, WHO WAS DISEASED WITH AN ISSUE (flow) OF BLOOD LASTING TWELVE YEARS. SHE CAME BEHIND JESUS, AND TOUCHED THE "**HEM OF HIS GARMENT**".

Even though she only reached the hem, **she said within herself** (she rehearsed the thought in her mind/soul) **that if she could just touch His Garment she would be whole** (well, preserved, entirely perfect). She would be cured of her problem of a continuous menstrual flow that had worn her down for twelve years.

Note, the woman touched the **Hem of His Garment**, but she spoke to herself (her body, soul, and spirit), the whole person. She involved every part of her being. She spoke to her mind, desire, will, emotions, passion, intellect, the very life of God within her, even her tired and hurting body and she said to **herself**; I've got to **Touch his Garment** and I will be totally well. She rehearsed the goal. She meditated on it causing her faith to be strengthened: if I could touch his garment, if I could touch his garment;

I will be whole, protected, and entirely healthy. She wanted to touch his garment believing she would be healed by doing this simple act of faith.

Although this woman, because of the great crowd around Jesus, was only able to touch the **HEM** of His garment, the Bible says Jesus turned about and when he saw her, he told her to be of good comfort (cheer) because her faith had made her completely well from that time forward.

The word *whole* in Biblical Greek means to be safe, saved, delivered, protected, healed, preserved, well, healthy, and perfect entirely. Derivatives of the word include even to have a wholesome tongue which speaks and declares deliverance, and a gentle tongue that is temperate thus turning away wrath and anger that could effect ones health and wholeness. Hallelujah! This woman, like many of us, was desperately tired of her situation and wanted to be perfect entirely and she did not stop, but persevered until she got what she wanted and needed from The Lord.

The central thought of this brief narrative is touching the garment and the hem of His garment. Allow your holy, redeemed, transformed intellect to generate two very strong questions that will be answered later: What was so important and powerful about the garment? What was so important and powerful about the hem of the garment that by touching a garment or a hem of a garment; a person could be healed emotionally, physically, financially, socially, and in every other aspect of her life? How could one touch completely and perfectly cause health and total deliverance?

CHAPTER FOUR

The Condition

For twelve years the woman in Matthew, chapter nine had searched for a cure for the illness in her body. Today, when women have a menstrual cycle and the blood flow is heavy for four or five days, maybe a few of those being light days; they are tired and glad when it's all over. They sometimes dread the pre-menstrual days when the cycle is even approaching.

Some women experience tension, bloating, back pain, headaches, excessive sweating; some experience diarrhea or constipation and/or regurgitation. Now, imagine twelve years of hemorrhaging, twelve straight years of being on a menstrual cycle. Losing blood makes one weak and anemic. Practically speaking it can be very expensive to provide the daily sanitary protection, which does not include whether an insurance or medical card carrier will or will not cover for a physician's diagnosis or treatment of the condition. A woman even needs more toiletries to keep the body clean, which includes utilities; and having clean water is mandatory. During this woman's historical times, who was there to help her to go draw water from the well? Did this woman work? How many of us if we work, have a package plan that will give us medical leave for twelve years, and how much will it cost to go to hospitals all over the city and country to get an answer or cure? Sometimes our circumstances press us so vigorously, that we have no choice other than to press in to get our miracle from the Lord.

In today's society physicians will maybe allow a woman to hemorrhage a few months. The advice after this ongoing condition would be a strong recommendation for a partial or full hysterectomy.

Among African –American women fibroid tumors are more common than in other races and are often the cause of an excessive flow of blood. Medications are prescribed to try to shrink the tumors to stop the flow, sometimes prothrombin, which coagulates the blood, or dosages of natural Vitamin K are administered.

At any rate twelve years of paying physicians, taking medications, purchasing sanitary pads or tampons for daytime protection and special pads for overnight, will drain your finances and cause your soul and spirit to be downcast, depressed and it could very well seem hopeless.

These were the conditions the woman in scripture had to endure, except there was no Playtex or Kotex in those days. You can imagine the hardship on women of Bible times. For twelve long years this woman looked for a cure for her condition. She was challenged in her body, soul, and spirit; and culturally, she was considered an outcast and compared to a leaper, a sinner. She had to announce her presence in the community when going from place to place.

The scripture does not speak on the source of the woman's livelihood. It could have been inheritance, or a returned dowry because of divorce. Whatever the case, she was desperate and had come to the end of her means/finances. She was determined to touch his garment, believing she would be made totally whole.

Most of the history in those days was handed down through storytelling and great value was placed upon tradition and religious practices. It is likely that the woman of Matthew nine had heard about whom Jesus was and his power to heal her. She had apparently known about the Aaronic and Levitical Priesthood practices from the previous generations of the Jews. She was aware of the value of the garments of the priesthood and even those who were assigned to make these meticulously designed garments. Although in her unclean condition, she knew she would be pushed away from Jesus by the crowd, she had the insight and faith to know that it would only take touching the hem of this Messiah's robe. After all, he was the one the old covenant fathers had prophesied about. The prophets of old foretold his coming.

This chapter closes with a review of the dimensions of man: body, soul, and spirit.

This woman needed to be made whole in her **body**, her physical being. It was the part of her that felt pain, needed food and shelter -- her flesh. She might have had a husband who left her because of the condition, so there would have been a physical void of the presence of someone being in her life for support. This kind of thing leaves a pain that reaches even into the realm of the soul.

Perhaps the area that is hardest for believers is the area of the **soul**. This is our emotions, our feelings, the mind, attitude, reasoning, and thinking, even our desires. There are many thoughts and feelings that go through a person's mind when so much time passes and a physical condition lingers. It can cause one's faith to waiver, but not in the case of the woman of Mathew nine. She pushed beyond the point of help for her condition, ignoring the conventional rules of caution.

Could it be that she had a wounded **spirit** after 12 years as she wondered why God allowed her to be in this situation? Had there been a decrease in her personal prayer time and worship of the Lord? We'll see in more detail how her spirit was effected as we look at the chapter on history, but it is safe to say that although this woman had suffered a tremendous amount of her life time, she managed to not close the door to her faith in God (the spiritual part of mankind) and her belief that God was still with her and would heal her whole person.

This is a key factor if you want God to make you whole; maintain a simple grain of faith that at some point the Lord will intervene and make you totally healthy. This belief penetrates beyond the condition of your body, to how you perceive life in your mind and what your will and desire are; this instigates a change in the realm of the spirit of mankind. All dimensions are impacted; then total healing is eminent. Your entire condition will change.

CHAPTER FIVE

The History

The woman of Matthew chapter nine had the kind of illness that carried with it a stigma of uncleanness. The Jews in Biblical times considered women unclean during menstruation and anyone who touched a woman during menstruation was made unclean until evening. If a woman continued to bleed beyond her normal cycle, she was considered unclean until the bleeding stopped. The rule was that it was the unclean person's responsibility to keep away from other people so as not to contaminate them. The impact on a person's self-esteem would be great. One would become the topic for neighborhood gossip, and of course few, if any friendships would remain in tact after 12 years.

This woman's desperation reached out beyond the comforts of man and even the rules and rituals of religion in order to touch the garment of God for her own healing. And God met her in her desperate moment. Can you imagine this woman coming through the crowd to touch the garment of Jesus to **be healed, to be delivered, preserved, and to be made well**?

I don't doubt that when some saw her they moved back for fear she would contaminate them because they knew their Jewish history -- the teachings of their fathers and forefathers. See Leviticus, chapter fifteen. I believe this woman had already suffered the gossip and talk of the neighborhood, and was maybe even known in surrounding communities because of the numbers of physicians she had sought for help; and people talk. Yet, she took the risk of more ridicule to come out in the thicket of crowds of people seeking Jesus, in order to reach him for her need.

CHAPTER SIX

Your Issue

God is calling each of us to ignore the risk factors of friends, family, culture and even those in our religious community, if they try to hinder us from moving to a deeper walk with him. This is not an endorsement to walk in rebellion with your church pastors and leadership; God means those bystanders who have no clue of what you and your pastors have been in counsel about. The opinions of man, and even the direct negative comments and accusations of those watching your life cannot begin to match the outcome of the blessings awaiting you when you obey God.

This woman's body needed healing, but her soul also needed healing. This means her mind; the way she thought about herself, had become affected because of the condition of her body. Her desires for living and life were challenged. Her emotions were at a near end. She had cried herself to sleep many times, perhaps even entertained suicide. She doubted if anyone really understood her condition, nor cared about her end result.

If she were of our time, perhaps she would have entertained backsliding, hanging out again with the wrong crowd – whoever would accept her in her condition. Perhaps she would have taken to clubs and bars trying to forget the pain, or playing destructive games with men and women in the church. She had already begun to wonder if God still loved her. She had suffered the stares and finger pointing and non-concealed whispering gossip of her so-called friends -- some sinners and some saints. Regardless, she refused to allow her spirit to be so wounded to the extent that she would not run to the source of her healing. That's the attitude God is saying we must have in order to walk in full deliverance, to be completely whole of the conditions that have been troubling us for years, even the things that we can hide from others, but not from ourselves nor God.

Some of you have been there and done that. You can identify with this great woman of scripture who was given no name. Maybe your issue is not blood, but the loss of a job thus creating a change of lifestyle for you and you're bitter because of the way you now have to live which is void of some luxuries you were used to, and you're waiting on God to move for you.

Maybe your husband left you or you finally left him after having had enough of what God never told you to take, but man kept you in bondage telling you to stay with that scoundrel; so you're still wondering how God is going to put the pieces of your life together again.

Maybe your issue is the spirit of depression and disappointment because your life is not going the way you planned it to go. You are a certain age and feel like the day is almost over to see your dream fulfilled and so you are soul sick and wounded in your spirit, feeling like your world is crushed.

Perhaps you have been hurt in the church and are tired of the church games played by leaders and members whose old lifestyle dominates their every thought, action and decision. Are pushed out because you can see it all clearly and will not play the games.

Maybe your issue is you decided to do it God's way and put your "baby's daddy" out of your apartment until he thinks you're worthy enough to publicly honor with marriage. Now you have the kids and he won't pay up and your body is missing the relationship, and your wounded soul causes you to wonder if you made the right decision, and your spirit is effected because your prayer life and your praise life is not the same causing your relationship with God to be on the back burner because of damage he has done.

Perhaps you are still slipping in the darkness and sleeping with the enemy by night and ashamed to let anyone know you are too weak to let him go.

Maybe your issue is you're just plain tired of doing the right thing all the time and refusing to bow to the images of this world, and your soul and spirit just needs encouragement and courage to stand and having done all to stand, keep standing.

Maybe your issue is for years you've allowed family and others to blame you for the behavior, decisions, and addictions of your children, therefore you're being eaten up with a false guilt and trying to make right and justify and heal things in your kids lives that only the Holy Spirit can heal. Or you might be the grandmother who is now rearing those children and suffering from all of the weight thereof.

Maybe your issue is you're dealing with the daggers of jealousy of Christians who don't know the price you paid to be where you are in Christ and seek to tear you apart in the mouths of others with gossip, the grapevine; and your struggle is to not hold anger or resentment or hurt against them.

Maybe your issue is you need to press through the crowd of religious opinion and break forth into the gifts and callings God has placed in you to be a blessing to the body. You've put yourself behind prison bars and you're uncomfortable because God is thrusting you out and you're allowing people to confine you.

Maybe your issue is God is saying get up and grow up, for too long you've just been slothful, depending on others, refusing to apply the word of God that you already have in you. You're running from one conference to the next, looking for one prophetic word after another, when the word of God to you for a long time has been get up and grow up. Get a job and keep it. Get 1-½ jobs, if you need to, get two to pay your bills. Stop being jealous and feeling sorry for yourself while others are enjoying life, because they've chosen to do what is required of them in this natural world. Let them be an example for you and do the same. Touch the garment of the Lord and let him give you strength to be godly men and women. It's your time to be a blessing to someone else, to begin to be a voice of counsel to someone coming the way God is bringing you.

Maybe your issue is physical: diabetes, renal failure, heart condition, hypertension, psoriasis, obesity, cancer, psychological disorders, tumors, or infertility. You can be made whole. Don't be foolish and ignore the natural laws of the land and blame God for your condition. Go to your doctor, your herbalist, and exercise. God is in all of that. Take the necessary vitamins and minerals beneficial for your blood type and avoid the foods that work against your natural blood type which cause toxins to develop in your body. Press through the crowd of your circumstances and be made whole!

Do not allow the frustrations of your issues to paralyze you. This is what the woman in Matthew chapter nine refused to do. Although every fiber of her body, soul, and spirit was challenged and tried, there was enough left in her spirit to know she needed to reach out to Jesus, and to touch him and only he could heal her entire being, so she did and so she was healed.

CHAPTER SEVEN

What was in the Garment?

Why was there such significance and faith in touching the garment? What was in the garment? What does that mean to us today?

Remember, the believers in the New Testament had the advantage of the rich history of their people from the Old Covenant. God mandated Israel to tell their children, and their children's children for each generation forever, about the way God delivered them. Story telling and the reading of the scrolls were common. The New Testament descendants of the early Jews were not strangers to the knowledge and practices of their ancestors, even though the followers of Christ were first called Christians at Antioch. This woman in Matthew, chapter nine knew about the history of her forefathers and how Aaron, the high priest wore an especially anointed robe. Scripture calls it the garment of the high priest.

God gave specific orders to Moses of how the Priest's garment was to be designed when he instructed the people of Israel to build The Tabernacle in the Wilderness. The orders for the design of the garments for the high priest were in these instructions. God specified the colors it should be made of, the colors of the thread and even the Mitre (the hat) and the breaches underneath, the names of the tribes on the shoulders and the stones of each tribe on the breastplate. The woman in Matthew knew that all the camp of Israel was centered on the Tabernacle of Moses and the activities of the priests and the High Priest. More importantly, this woman knew of the prophesies of the coming of the Great High Priest, Jesus, who would be the wonderful counselor, the mighty God, the everlasting Father, the Prince of Peace. She knew that everything in the Old Testament Priesthood was a shadow or example of things to come, and represented something God was going to do in the New Testament and also in future generations.

Specific instructions were given for making the garments. Read Exodus chapters 28 – 39. Focus specifically on chapters 31, 32 and 39 for instructions on the robe of the ephod. It was to be woven all blue and with a hole in the center like the hole of a habergeon (which means a breast-plate of armor) designed so it could not be rent or torn. This was significant of the unchanging love of Christ and his firm hand in our lives that neither death, nor persecution, nor things present nor things to come can separate us from loving him and likewise, nothing can pluck us from his hand. He has formed a breastplate of armor about us declaring that no weapon formed against us can hurt us. He has established a covenant with us that cannot be rent, torn, or broken.

The Old Testament term for robe in the Hebrew was **mantle**, as in a garment worn by a king. It is also translated as **cloak**. The color blue signifies the color worn by the Heavenly King. It typified the Christ that was to come as the heavenly king who would save his people from their sins. This is who the woman in Matthew was reaching out to. He was Jesus, The Great Shepherd, the Prince of Peace, and the King of Righteousness. What does this mean to us? We also, just as the woman in Matthew reached for the cloak or garment of Jesus realizing he could make her whole, should reach to Jesus realizing that we are reaching for and to the Heavenly King who makes us whole. We are reaching out to the one who came from heaven down. This robe was to cover the high priest from head to foot, stipulating that when the Great High Priest comes, he would come from the heavens. The blue color typified how he humbled himself to be like humankind on earth so that he could pay the full price for sin and fully redeem mankind.

The woman in Matthew was saying, as she struggled to reach the robe of Jesus, that she acknowledged him as the Great High Priest, the King of Righteousness, The Prince of Peace, the Great Shepherd that had come down from heaven, the one spoken of by her ancestors (Is. 9:6 – Unto us a child is born, a son is given and the government and authority will be upon his shoulder and his name will be called Wonderful, Counselor, Mighty God, Everlasting Father, Prince of Peace). This is why this nameless woman could have such great faith. She was not reaching from the perspective of a shallow view of the *rumor* of a man named Jesus coming to town. She was reaching to the historical, cultural and religious person of the Messiah who was prophesied as the coming King and Savior of the Jews who was sent from God who would heal and deliver those who believed.

We agree that our king has come and we need only to reach out to him and by faith, we are made completely well in our body, our soul, and our spirit. In the original language the word *whole* means we are healed, delivered, preserved, made well, saved, and we speak wholeness with our tongue and gentleness which is the law of life that releases fountains of deliverance upon us and others, even from those ISSUES that have held us captive for years.

When Jesus told the woman that faith had made her well, he was speaking of a faith in the true God she had believed in since the history of her childhood, who was actually *now* walking the earth and was available for her to receive from his mantle, his cloak, his robe, his garment. When she said to herself she wanted to touch his garment, perhaps she even called to her memory the story from her forefathers that told of the double portion that Elisha received from Elijah's mantle. She knew she needed a powerful touch from Jesus. She believed and received her healing; so can we.

We in this Covenant are more privileged than the woman in Matthew chapter nine, because a physical Jesus was her target. She had to touch him while he was passing through the town in order to receive her blessing. We reach to a Christ who is omniscient and omnipresent (knows all and is everywhere). He is Spirit (John 4:24). There are no boundaries, no tangible crowds, no limitations, and no hindrances to our touching him. We too reach out by faith and are candidates to receive the miracles and wonders of the Messiah, the King of the Kingdom, Lord and Savior, the Christ, the Son of the living God.

CHAPTER EIGHT

What is in the Hem?

T he woman in Matthew nine could not grasp hold to the robe, although it was in her heart to do, but she was able to touch just the **Hem** of his robe. What was the significance of the hem? The Greek word for *hem* means the margin, a fringe, tassel, or a boarder. It is also translated, as the skirts of his garment (Jeremiah 13, 22-26). In Isaiah chapter six, it is translated as the train of his garment.

The historical and traditional boarder or hem of the garment was not only trimmed in the heavenly **blue**, symbolic of our right to approach the **God of the heavens** for our deliverance, but the fringe or hem of the priest's garment was lined with **blue** and **purple** and **scarlet pomegranates and bells of gold** between them (Exodus 28:33–35).

The blue, purple and scarlet pomegranates on the High Priest's robe symbolized that the priest was coming before God as a mere earthly man from the world below; just as the **fruit of the pomegranates on his robe were gathered from the earth** below. This means that when we come asking the Lord for a miracle, we must realize that we are mere earthly men in the light of his glorious power and presence. Yet, we are made and covered by the blood of Jesus (scarlet), therefore we qualify as his heirs and joint heirs and we have a right to healing for our body, soul, and spirit. The Bible boasts of the manner of love the Father has placed upon us that we are called the sons of God (1 John 3:l). Therefore, we don't come indignant as his servants, but we do come boldly to the throne of grace to find help in the time of need as his heirs.

Remember, it was God, himself, who spoke to Moses telling him exactly how the priest's robe must be designed. So, the Father was saying this is a **pattern for my people concerning healing for generations to come**. The Old Covenant High Priest was a direct picture of the coming Christ who would be our New Covenant High Priest, the mediator between God and man, Jesus Christ the righteous (1 Timothy 2:5). This Christ was the high priest the woman of Matthew touched. It was the **hem of HIS** garment that contained all the healing power and authority of the Old Covenant (OT) High Priest; even greater because the OT priest was a mere shadow of the true substance that would come in the Messiah, Jesus.

We reach out and touch the blue, purple, and scarlet fruit (pomegranates) on the fringe, the boarder of his garment: **blue**, represents the manifestation of God as the one who showed so great a love that he came from the father in heaven down to sacrifice his life for us by way of the death of the cross.

Purple, represents the manifestation of the **God-man**, and supports the great mystery of Godliness. The color symbolizes royalty throughout scripture and speaks to us in this text as God who was manifested in the flesh through his son Jesus, justified in the spirit, and received into glory. There can't be any royalty more deserving of honor than the king of glory. And who is this king of glory? He is the Lord strong and mighty, the Lord mighty in battle, and the Lord of Hosts. Lift up you head O ye gates, the gates of your heart, and this king of glory will come into your scene, the situation in your life and make you whole (Ps. 24:9).

Scarlet fruit represents the manifestation of the true dignity and glory of **the man, Christ**, the glory that was seen in the Lord Jesus Christ the **son of man**, that he chose to suffer, hurt, bleed, and die as a mere earthly man in order to redeem man back to the Father. He shed innocent blood. He would not come down from the cross, but was beaten, scourged, and died for us. With his stripes, we were healed. This gives us the right to push through any crowd of circumstances in order to receive wholeness for our body, our soul and spirit, the pneuma – which is that part of us that meets with the spirit of God and creates life. It's by the blood/scarlet that was poured out for us.

This pomegranate fruit on the hem or boarder of the high priest's garment also represents to us, the fruit of the spirit: love, joy, peace, long-suffering, gentleness, goodness, faith, meekness, and temperance. Being carriers of this fruit is the only way we can expect to receive anything from the Lord.

These pomegranates represent the FRUIT of the spirit (singular), because each one of these graces is dependent upon and connected to the other. If you don't have any joy, you cannot have peace and neither can you really love anyone with the agape love and show gentleness and temperance. Accordingly, without these you won't be healed or made whole entire and healthy. The Bible says a merry heart is good, like a medicine to the body. This woman wanted what was in the hem, which is fruitfulness, joy, peace, restored, and life. Even so, because of what she had gone through **she knew better than many others the need for love, joy, peace, long suffering, gentleness, goodness, faith, meekness, and temperance.** She had learned to minister these fruit to others because she knew what it was to not have them. Her infirmity made her a greater minister of his word and his power to deliver others because he had delivered her to shalom. The crowd of circumstances could not hold her back, and we cannot permit anything to hold us back.

There is always a crowd of circumstances that will cluster to try to prevent or block you from receiving your healing. Determine what is keeping you from believing and receiving. Push past those obstacles and touch the Lord to receive the blue, purple and scarlet fruit (the pomegranate) for yourself. Let nothing stop you from touching the God of the heavens, the royal King of Kings, the one who shed his blood purchasing your redemption and enabling the fruit of the spirit to not only be experienced personally, but to be an able minister to pour these fruit upon others. The fulfilled promises that are yours are worth pressing through and past the crowd of circumstances.

CHAPTER NINE

The Golden Bells? What's that Sound?

L et us close with the golden bells that were attached to the hem of the High Priest's garment between the pomegranates. Exodus, chapters 24 and 25 are recommended readings that bring further understanding to this chapter. What is the meaning of the bells?

The woman with the issue of blood was reaching out to the Lord to reclaim the song in her heart! She wanted desperately to be able to worship in the camp of God again. According to Jewish culture, a woman on her menstrual cycle was excluded from participating in the life and worship that took place in the community of the believers.

The woman longed to be in the fellowship with God and his people. David said we are to speak to ourselves in psalms, hymns, and spiritual songs, and this singing and making melody in our hearts to the Lord would deliver us (Eph. 5:19). He also instructed the people to have a song in the night or during difficult times in life (Ps. 77:6). David even shared how there were times in his life when he had to think himself happy creating a spiritual elevation in his own mind that was higher than the circumstances that he was facing when he was being accused by King Agrippa (Acts 26:2).

This chapter nine woman followed these instructions from the scrolls of the book of Psalms. Yet, there came a time when she needed the assembly, the gathering of the people to be strengthened and sustained and her condition was prohibiting this. Any time a condition becomes so powerful in your life that it effects your worship, it's time to take a stand and trample over it and whatever obstacles that get in your way in order to receive what you need from the Lord; your healing, your deliverance. It's the time to be like a pit bull and lock your spiritual teeth into what you need and refuse to let go until you get what is needed. To cut off corporate worship is to sever part of what gives you life. Just think, twelve years with no fellowship. She knew she had to re-claim the worship in her heart and fellowship with believers, which was essential to relationship and life.

When the high priest of Biblical days would walk in and out of the glory of God in the camp of Israel, a melodious sound was always heard. It was the sound of love, peace, joy and praise to an awesome God who was doing awesome things for his people. It was to be a heavenly melody ringing out in the presence of God in the camp. The instructions from God were that the sound of the bells on the skirt of the Priest's garment were to be heard when the priest went in the holy place before the Lord so that he would not die (Exodus 24 – 26). If you allow your circumstances to keep you from the house of God, to keep you from making your sound of praise unto the Lord in the gathering of the saints and in the presence of the Lord, you will eventually die, spiritually.

This death may not be a physical death, although it could be, but it will certainly be a wilting away of your soul and a spiritual death. God commands us to praise him, and to assemble ourselves together with the brethren to offer corporate praise and worship (Heb. 10:25). There is something about coming into the house of God with a made up mind to sing and praise God no matter what is going on around you. That praise and worship will assist with your deliverance. Also, part of one's healing is sometimes in the songs and words of encouragement received from other believers and God's preached word. It is always worth it to travel where ever you need to travel to get to a place where genuine praise and worship is occurring, where the sound of the bells in God's presence is heard.

The Bible declares that the sound that goes out from Zion (the church) should be the saints of God praising his name, declaring the Lord is good and his mercy endures forever (Ps. 105: 5). God was not interested in the sound of complaining, the sound of gossip, the sound of strife and contention in the sanctuary; but the sound of praise, the sound of worship, and the sound of giving thanks and the sound of giving. This was the sound of the bells that was to be heard from the Holy of Holies from the hem of the priest's garment and the presence of the Lord. Likewise, this is the sound we are to make in the house of God. What's that sound? It is a sweet melody of song and praise unto the Lord from our earthly mouths, we must take unto our Lord, our King the fruit of our lips which is giving thanks and praise to Him – our bells and pomegranate. To receive your healing, you must become a worshipper. You must not let your circumstance no matter how difficult it is, smother the sound of the bells of worship. Like the woman in Matthew, reach out to re-claim the sound of worship in your mouth and in the sanctuary of the corporate gathering of believers. The sound of praise should continually flow from your mouth, even in the core of your pain. This is one of the prescriptions to receive God's healing.

The color *gold* is a type of Divine Glory seen in the Lord Jesus as the Son of God. It was shadowed in the Old Testament as a type of God, himself. When you start allowing your voice of praise and worship to be heard as a sound, a sweet melody before him giving praise to the divine and holy one, you're going to get results! Your spirit is going to be renewed. Life is going to come as you sound your own golden bells of praise and worship to the divine King of Glory. Your circumstances and issues, what ever they are, will become small in the light of his Glory and the power of God to change your circumstances or to change you while walking through your circumstances.

Recognizing His divinity in your life will place into proper perspective your humanity. He has the power to change all things. The splendor and power of our King causes everything and everyone to rank inferior to his superior might. Jesus is the King of Glory, the Lord strong and mighty, the God to whom we direct our sound, the bells -- our worship.

CHAPTER TEN

Epilogue

The woman with the issue of blood had a history of knowledge, revelation, and instruction that let her know the significance of grasping the garment, the robe, the mantle, the cloak of Jesus. She knew he was the manifestation of what her forefathers had seen only in shadows, types, and examples. Not only did she know what was in the garment, she knew what was even in the fringes, the boarder, and the hem of the garment. Her faith was concrete because of her foundation. It's no surprise that Jesus turned to her because he felt (virtue) power leave his body. Her faith pulled and reached and tugged from generations past to proclaim, Jesus as the Christ, the Living God whose power could make her whole, delivered and preserved, well, and healed. Her faith caused the condition of her body to align with what God had appropriated concerning her life. And she was healed. The Lord told her that her faith had caused her healing.

Your history as a believer, a follower of Christ, is as potent as the woman of Matthew, chapter 9. I pray this simple piece of literature will give you knowledge, revelation, instructions, and understanding that will provide a concrete foundation for your faith to make you whole in your body, your soul and in your spirit. Jesus told the woman her faith had made her whole. Be healed.

FROM PRESS TO PASSION
and
The Creature is Grumbling

(Adjusting Your View of Kingdom Advancement)

Introduction

I was once talking in a phone conversation with a dear friend of mine in the ministry. As we were encouraging one another in the ministry, she made a statement that captured my heart; it really sank deep into my heart and thoughts long after our conversation had ceased. She spoke of God moving believers from a place of *press* to *passion*. Although she made the statement once, it must have resounded over and over in my spirit for several days. As I prayed concerning the statement for myself first, and for the people of God to whom my husband and I minister, the Holy Spirit began to give me illumination and understanding of truth he wanted me to embrace and share with believers. Thus, this section of Kingdom Quest was birthed.

My prayer is that you will be blessed as you read this work and that you will be inspired to move into an ambit of passion for the Lord and the Kingdom of God that lies far beyond the level of labor and struggle. As a recipient of the truth of this reading, I pray you are propelled to a place from *Press* to *Passion* as you understand creatures and creation are grumbling and moaning for you to manifest your gifts, calling, and purpose on earth as a Son of the living God.

CHAPTER ONE

His Plan

In this era we are living in there is a demand to intensify, accelerate, move in full throttle and deeper commitment to whatever it is that one says he or she needs and loves. Most employers are even requiring more productivity in the work field, yet compensating employees with the same pay or less pay prior to the increased work load.

While this precipice of unrest and struggle is occurring in the natural, the Lord is moving the body of Christ **from** a place of struggling, intensifying, and accelerating **laboriously**, **to** a place of moving forward with joy, passion, enthusiasm, ardor, devotion, affection, loyalty, and zeal! The difference is that our actions will yield results of personal victory and spiritual triumph! These results will impact the church in a manner that establishes "kingdom" authority and rule which automatically propels believers to a level of power that will impact our communities and the world! This is the plan of the Lord as believers operate in passion for his purpose rather than proceed in life struggling and stressing, thus poorly positioned to be candidates to be used to help His Kingdom to come and His Will to be done on earth.

While this acceleration and aggression is happening in the systems of the world, without compensation for effort, the plan of the Lord is that his sons and daughters who go forth <u>with passion</u> will receive compensation, reward, and restitution for all we invest into the kingdom of God.

While the economy and the natural disasters in the world, and wars and rumors of wars, and crime and family disturbances seem to be screaming "all is falling apart"; the voice of the Lord and the pulse of the heart of the Father is saying, just draw near to me, don't dilute, but concentrate your relationship with me because there is a more abounding grace that exists in the earth than the chaos and calamity that you see with the natural eye. The power and authority of his true Church of God is prevailing.

The Lord's grace is in full throttle ready to abound much more than calamity so that the church and the world sees, in the center of the chaos, the demonstration of power and might from his prepared sons and daughters as they go forward with the joy and passion that will usher in His glory on a greater level! Don't dilute, become more potent in your passion for Christ and Kingdom work. Follow his plan. God wants to take believers from exertion to rest, from labor to favor, from vacillation to motivation, from hesitation to inspiration, from irresolution to certainty, from hesitation to stimulation, from **press to passion**!

CHAPTER TWO

The Earth is Waiting – The Creature

Moving from an attitude of press to an attitude of passion will revivify your entire life. It doesn't matter if you are pursuing your relationship with the Lord, your dreams, your calling, your goals, or your relationships with others; you will surely change and so will the people in your sphere of influence. There will be a difference in your personal and corporate prayer, in personal and corporate worship, in service to the Lord, in how you view placement on your job, in commitments, views about evangelism, structures and foundations in your life, and organizations you are part of. Your personal life, businesses, and family will be revived when you adjust your view of kingdom advancement with passion for a cause rather than labor and pressing merely to accomplish a task.

A believer performing what he or she does in love, peace, enthusiasm, and joy while understanding God's purpose, will move into a place where he or she is a candidate for the manifested glory and miracles God desires to release in the earth. The earth is groaning and grumbling for us believers (creatures) to manifest the power of God now! This cannot happen if our life is one of pressing, laboring ahead, moving drudgingly along, painfully pushing ahead, doing what we do in an agonizing manner, and feeling distressed and stressed about the work of the Lord and the responsibilities we have committed to do in the house of the Lord. The Bible states that the very earth is waiting on you and me – the powerful sons and daughters of the Lord to manifest his glory! A passion for Him, His presence, and His work is the only way power and authority become visible and manifested through us. This *dynamos* power can happen in and on the earth and is available from the Lord through us.

The Apostle Paul stated:

> Romans 8:19 - For the earnest <u>expectation</u> of the <u>creature</u> waiteth for the **manifestation** of the **sons of God**.

The word *expectation* in this scripture comes from a compound word in the Greek that means a sense of intense watching and anticipation. It further means an earnest looking forward to something. So, who is honestly looking forward to and intensely watching and anticipating the manifestation of the sons of God? The scripture states that the creature is in expectation, waiting. What is meant by the word *creature*?

The word *creature* in this scripture means <u>literally or figuratively, a building</u>. Literally, a building is a physical structure made of some solid substance that enables it to stand. **Figuratively and symbolically,** a <u>building is spoken of as a</u> <u>human being, mankind, a man or woman or child.</u> Repeatedly the Bible uses this kind of symbolic reference. So, we can safely conclude from the fore-mentioned scripture that physical buildings are literally waiting, shaking in expectation, hoping for God's manifested glory that is resident in believers, to stabilize the chaos on planet earth. The creature (the literal buildings) is expecting us to rise in the might and power of our God and have a more positive impact on planet earth!

The scripture is actually personifying *creature* as a literal building. Human beings -- the figurative meaning of *creature* -- are earnestly looking forward to, anticipating, watching intensely for the manifestation of the sons of God! People on the earth want to see changes in our world, our society, our communities, our schools, our governments; but the forces needed to bring about change can only be activated by God's anointed army of kingdom builders manifesting son-ship. When we manifest our individual son-ship on earth and demonstrate his gifts as a mighty army of the Lord, then conditions on earth will change.

The word *creature* in Romans 8:19 also (in its basic Greek meaning) implies <u>creation</u> such as: **mountains, hills, rivers, trees, heavenly bodies, creature life forms, organisms, human beings as creatures, living beings, animals, and beasts or insects.** All of these forms of creation are waiting for the manifestation of the sons of God! The Bible speaks of trees of the fields clapping and mountains bowing! Can we think enough like God to conceive that the calamities of the earth are representation that a powerful move of God needs to be seen on the earth in order to command the elements to be still as Christ commanded the sea to calm? Yes, mighty and unusual kinds of miracles are occurring on earth in some places, but the creature is crying for an increase, even greater manifestation.

It is conceivable and emphatically stated as we study God's word, that when believers of Jesus **pursue him with passion** and joy and create an atmosphere and an environment conducive for him to move in his majesty and in miracles, then change will take place in the lives of humans and all creation and creatures on planet earth!

Seeking him in agony and distress, pressing or laboring in our service to him because of duty and mere responsibility, will not prepare the way for the manifestation of the power of God. Consequently, such an outpouring of power will result from us seeking him and **following after him like the deer longs for the water and flowing with him in devotion, affection, passion, loyalty, ardor, and love. This will revivify our lives, our communities, and our world! Passion for His purpose will lead us to this level of manifestation of His power and glory!**

The word *creature* in Romans 8:19 furthermore **means ordinances** such as **regulations, edicts, rules, laws, verdicts, judgments, pronouncements, and declarations.** Therefore we can in summary, conclude with illuminated insight that buildings literally and figuratively; broken distorted criminals and habit addicted human buildings, twisted politicians, buildings in sexual identity crisis, racially obtuse thinkers, lost and hurting teens, homeless and helpless citizens, hospitalized disillusioned patients, are all waiting for the believers, the sons of God to manifest the power and glory of God in the earth!

Furthermore, we can conclude that mountains, rivers, trees, heavenly bodies, creature life forms, organisms, human beings as creatures, animals, and beasts and insects, waters and oceans, are all saying, sons of God come establish order, rescue the earth! Manifest the glory, power and beauty of His presence on earth! We are in earnest expectation, we are groaning for your manifestation!

Furthermore, we are certain that laws and rules, regulations, edicts, verdicts, judgments, pronouncements, and declarations are saying sons of God come and set the books straight; for the government shall be upon His shoulders and He is the Wonderful Counselor, the Might God, the Everlasting Father, The Prince of Peace! And the law shall go forth out of Zion and the word of the Lord from Jerusalem, from the city and called out people of God!

I say to you Sons of God, we are Zion! We are Jerusalem! Manifest the Glory of The Lord in the earth! The creature is waiting and is in earnest expectation of the sons of God's to <u>manifest the power of God in the earth</u> – the power of the divine, supreme magistrate! To manifest means to appear, to lighten, to reveal, express and demonstrate! This is the call, the challenge, the responsibility of the believers both old and young. Demonstrate your gifts and abilities by faith in the power of God within you; manifest as a son of the living God. Arise to the place of walking in your assigned destiny, the purpose given unto you since before the foundation of the world. The creature and creation are grumbling about our listlessness. Arise Zion, believers, Church of God, Kingdom agents! The set time of your favor has come (Ps. 102:13)! Manifest sons of the living God, heirs of salvation!

CHAPTER THREE

Linking Your Past to His Plan

In order to move forward with God in passion, there are some responsibilities we must embrace. We must surrender what we consider valuable in capitulation to God's idea, God's plan for our lives. That plan is to first know him, to strengthen relationship with him, to experience him in our lives, and to nurture our bond with our Savior and Lord. Are you willing to lose some things in order to gain a deeper experience with Christ? Once obtaining that deeper, more intimate relationship with the Creator, it is inevitable that one will experience the power, the force, the might, the influence, the anointing of his resurrection authority. Then you will be able to move and flow in that same life giving, resurgence, and power; thus you become a conduit that gives life to others, a channel through which the life of the Holy Spirit flows!

Another responsibility that we have to accept is forgetting the tragedies of our past that cause us to function in a mode of laboring and struggling in the matters of God. We must exchange these old ideas for those that foster views that are for the advancement of the kingdom of God. Adopt a position of love, ardor, joy, and passion.

God does not expect us to erase from our memory everything that has happened to cause pain in our lives. We are to place our past pain in proper perspective. To see the past from a distorted perspective is positioning the past as a picture of failure. It is damaging to healthy growth; but to see the past as a path you had to take in order to bring you to a greater and stronger and more triumphant future is a Kingdom advancement perspective!

Adjust the scenery of past experiences in your life so that whatever the scenes were, or whoever the actors were in the play are irrelevant; but, what's important is the fact that your scenery is a backdrop of light, love, hope, purpose, and the tapestry upon which everything else is drawn. The scenery of any dramatic presentation can either make or break the performance! It can cause the actors and actresses to seem effective or non-effective. It can cause positive light to shine on a character whose persona was dark and drab. Adjust the scenery of your past experiences so that your backdrop controls what the audience sees, so that when you look back upon your life's story you see light, love, hope, and purpose as the tapestry upon which pieces of the story of your life were drawn regardless of the flaws and intents of the actors. It is not an entire picture of who you are or where you are going. It contributes to making the powerful, confident, successful person that you are now. Forget those things behind you that seemed destructive; put them in proper perspective and see them as building and shaping platforms that made a stronger you because all things work for your good (Phil. 3:13, Rom. 8:28). This thinking will cause you to live more effectively in every area of your life. Moreover, this will encourage and impel your personal pursuit to know Christ more deeply and to serve him even more passionately.

This is what the Apostle Paul states:

> Philippians 3:7-13 Howbeit what things were gain to me, these have I counted loss for Christ. Yea verily, and I count all things to be loss for the excellency of the knowledge of Christ Jesus my Lord: for whom I suffered the loss of all things, and do count them but refuse, that I may gain Christ. And be found in him, not having a righteousness of mine own ... That I may know him, and the power of his resurrection, and the fellowship of his sufferings, becoming conformed unto his death; **(I'm willing to go through some things and even lose some things that I may win/know Him).** Not that I have already obtained, or am

already made perfect: but I press on. (*I push stringently forward, laboriously with toil*). Brethren, I count not myself yet to have laid hold: (apprehended) one thing I do, **forgetting the things which are behind** and stretching forward to the things which are before (my future).

Isn't that a powerful scripture for believers to life by? Nothing in your past was a failure or mistake; it all became a learning experience to make you and shape you to be the candidate that you are now, for God to use. Count your past as a joyful place and look to your future. Create your future with the choices you make in your present. Sure, there are some times when you will have to *press* and continue in a toiling manner, with arduous energy and labor. That is moving ahead in spite of your pain; however, that state, that condition, that position and attitude should <u>NOT be the norm for believers</u>! It should be the atypical situation, the uncommon the unusual! Our typical approach must be one of joy, passion, and gleeful expectation and service to the Lord.

Don't even permit your life to circulate around the good times in your past! Create good times in your present and determine your future by making appropriate and wise choices in your present. Believers, whose conversation is largely focused on what has already happened, are not believers who are creating their positive future. They are allowing random situations and circumstances to dictate their future based on a thoughtless remark that may have come in repeated or past conversation. Some individuals make it a practice to rehearse negative events that took place years ago. There are usually few present joys in this kind of person's life, thus there will be few future joys. We must be determined to keep our past in perspective, refusing to live in the past, but undergoing a paradigm shift to live in and shape our future, our destiny, our purpose for living and Kingdom advancement.

We have often visited congregations of believers where the worship was laborious, toiling, and where those serving in the church seemed unhappy, upset, distressed, hurt, and even angry while performing a responsibility in the house of God. In contrast, we have visited congregations where the worship was like living water flowing, the people were serving with gladness, a smile, joy, passion, and the love and peace of God was radiating from their faces. Which believers would you say please God most, although he can receive both when the heart is pure? The latter example of course is more pleasing. Passion is the source of motivation, inspiration, liberation, joy and celebration, which surges the believer with the power and might necessary to manifest as sons of God in the earth today. This is the plan of God for believers.

The Bible states in the book of Jeremiah that God's thoughts are for your peace, welfare and your success and that his plans are to bring you to an expected end. In the Hebrew, the words *expected end* mean there is a cord or attachment tied between you and God (figuratively). That bonding and connection is like a link or hook between you and your creator. This cord will give you hope and cause you to have the things he desires to come to pass in your life. So, The Lord has an expectation of what you are to develop into, and a cord is tied between his expectation and yours like a hook and an umbilical lifeline link. This supernatural connection will cause all wholeness concerning your past, present, and future to flow to you when your expectation parallels to his plan for you (Jeremiah 29:11).

This chapter will close with the Apostle Paul's words:

> Philippians 3:14 ... forgetting things behind ... I **press** toward the mark for the prize of the high **calling** of God in Christ Jesus.

The meaning of the Greek word *press* in this scripture means to ensue or follow laboriously with toil, stringent, suffering and persecution, to push down, compress with force or pressure. The word "calling" in this scripture has the basic Greek meaning of a high invitation, a calling to invite the highest level of guests from a divine, supreme magistrate! The Lord, the supreme magistrate, is calling you and me inviting us to a higher level in him.

The Anointed One wants to manifest through us. Press and struggle is necessary sometimes, but passion should be a lifestyle -- one that believers must live in order to be world changers, and life re-arrangers, in an era wherein Christ wants to move through his people at a level of passion that will impact creation, and the creature, piercing the ordinary atmosphere with an extraordinary anointing. This extraordinary anointing upon you will settle chaos, bring about deliverance, and radiate with a prevailing glory that proclaims The Lord Jesus Christ as King of Kings, Master, the only Divine, Supreme, Magistrate, Creator and Ruler of all things!

Paul's passion was to bear down, toil, and labor to know Christ, to be invited into the company of the supreme magistrate – Christ Jesus. His cry was for relationship and he was willing to toil, lay down whatever he had to lay aside in order to be in the presence, the company of the King. This he considered to be the highest calling, business, and mission at hand. It was the most important kind of race of all the game competitions during the culture of his time and it yielded the greatest prize.

Yes, sometimes we may labor to enjoy God's presence, but the typical approach should be simply resting in the presence and company of the King. We have a more excellent covenant where veils and special protocol and not mandated. Access is available based on the blood covenant of God's dear son, Jesus Christ. So we come boldly and with joy as we walk with our God because he is omnipresent, we enjoy living in his presence and experiencing the abundant life he promised.

The thing you want most, the thing you need, the thing you long for first, should be to know HIM and to walk with HIM and to be like HIM! From that true bonded relationship with Christ springs every other need and desire in life. When you fulfill your purpose in him, your destiny in every area of your life will make you whole: your career, your successful child-rearing, your marriage, your healing, your worship, your deliverance, your miracle, a healthy community, salvation for your family and friends, and so much more. All these things hinge upon your relationship with Christ – linking your past to His Plan!

CHAPTER FOUR

The Perfect Example

J esus was the chief example of exemplifying passion and joy. He was God who chose to wrap himself in flesh and come to earth and shed his precious blood in order to redeem us, to purchase us back to God after man fell into sin in the Garden of Eden. Jesus chose to endure the cruelty of the crucifixion because he had in mind that there would be generations of us, mankind, who would benefit from his sacrifice; so he freely gave his life demonstrating the ultimate love and passion for us. Joy was his approach. This is the recording in the scripture:

> Hebrews 12:2 ... looking unto Jesus the author and perfecter of *our* faith, who for the **joy** that was set before him endured the cross, despising shame, and hath sat down at the right hand of the throne of God.

The word *joy* in that passage has its root in the Hebrew word meaning: fervor, infatuation, excitement, zeal, blithesome glee, pleasure, jump, and exult for joy, cry out as a shout of triumph! Doesn't that change the perspective on what was really happening as he moved forward through the worst persecution and torture known to humans of his time? Jesus seemed sad, in great pain, distress, agony, and he was feeling these things in his flesh; yet, because of the passion and joy, pleasure, triumph and zeal that he felt, knowing he was giving us a future through redemption -- he endured the cross although his present human flesh did not like the shameful position and condition he was in at the time (Heb. 12:2).

He knew he was not only creating his future because he knew he would be resurrected and would return to the Father, he was also creating a future for generations of God's creation who would come after him. After he returned and was seated at the right hand of the Father, do you think he looked back on his past with sadness and grief, and pressed his way to be the mediator for us? Absolutely not! He looks back at the scene on Golgatha Hill as it is painted on a beautiful tapestry of glory and light and love and patience and surrender and hope. It was just one scene in his life; he is now the only mediator between God and man and is enthroned with The Father, full of glory!

The same word *joy* in the form of the word used in Hebrews 12:2, is mentioned over 165 times in the Bible. The word *press* in the reference in Philippians is mentioned only one to three times throughout the Bible! Then, how much more often is God speaking to his people about joy rather than struggle and labor? In this era, God is taking us from press to passion, labor to favor, unrest to peace, hesitation to motivation, upset to rest, and labor to ardor so that we can manifest the glory of God in the earth advancing the Kingdom!

It's time for the people of God to make the shift from press to passion in every area of our lives. The atmosphere in this epoch will not allow us to stay in the dimension of the press. We will die there. It will almost literally kill us because **we were designed for passion, rest, peace, and joy!**

CONCLUDING THOUGHTS

1) When Christ was on earth he did miracles not as God; but as a man submitted to the commands of his Father and the government of the Holy Ghost. Likewise, we are submitted to the commands of our Heavenly Father and the government of Holy Ghost. According to the scriptures, we will do great exploits in the earth through our God.

2) We are men and women of power designed for passion to manifest our purpose, gifts, callings, and the authority of God before man, the creature, and creation. We must fulfill our purpose and destiny in the earth; not pressing and toiling laboriously, but walking in our places as the sons of God in passion, joy, and authority!

3) The Woman with the issue of blood had to prevail through the crowd, being stepped on and pushed and weakened even more by the thick energy of the crowd, but she finally was able to get through to touch Jesus. The Bible states that Jesus felt her faith through her touch. He asked who touched him. His level of sensitivity and discernment enabled him to feel her fragile touch even in the middle of a curious crowd. Jesus told her that her faith had made her whole. She connected with the blue, purple, scarlet, pomegranates, and bells; the heavenly and royal King who paid for our life's freedom with his own blood enabling us to partake of the fruit of the spirit and worship unto our God with the congregation of the righteous.

Today the Lord says, we don't have to live a lifestyle of strain and struggling, we need only to move in joy, passion, love, and desire. Just as the woman's faith under the old covenant rules made her completely healed; in this new and better covenant the believer's faith will make us whole and completely healed!

Scripture does not say Jesus made her whole. It was her faith and passion to reach and touch Jesus that drove her through a crowd. This made her whole! Today's believers don't have a literal crowd to push through to reach him. We reach him with our passion in worship and service, through our words, our attitude of joy in living for him, our times of pursuing him and speaking with him in prayer; and our faith will grant us whatever we need and want. When we are whole, we are able to coach others into becoming whole; we impact our world for Christ.

4. Passion caused the woman with the alabaster box, 7 days before Jesus' burial, to break a box with a year's salary of oils and ointments and pour them on Jesus' feet worshipping him. His name is like ointment poured forth. Hallelujah! The only hope for America is your pouring forth the salve and balm of the power, deliverance, healing, help, hope, peace, of the Holy Sprit into the thirsty earth today. You, my beloved believer, sons of God, must move from press and struggle to joy and passion. You are an apothecary pouring healing and delivering ointment forth for the Master, the Mighty Magistrate, the Lord whom we have not seen, yet we love; whom although we cannot see him yet be believe and we rejoice with joy unspeakable and full of glory; knowing he is taking the labor and struggle from us replacing it with peace, hope, patience and the power of the Holy Spirit working within us to do of his good pleasure.

We are to manifest his power through his deposit of gifts, callings, charisma and abilities God placed in us to answer the grumbling call of the creature and creation as they wait on us allow God to flow through us, the believer, you, the Church, God's Kingdom agents.

Books Published By The Authors
Drs. Michael & Cecilia Jackson

1. 9 Gifts of the Holy Spirit
2. A Synopsis: Differentiating Religion, Tradition, Church, & Kingdom
3. A Woman's Heart
4. Be Made Whole
5. Belonging
6. Beyond The Veil
7. Bold Truth
8. Breaking The Curse of Poverty
9. Get Her Back on Her Feet
10. Categorizing Spiritual Gifts
11. Dialogue Between the Watchmen and The King
12. Discern Deploy The "Heir" Force
13. Dominion For Practical Singles
14. Don't Feed The Bears
15. Finding The RIGHT Woman
16. From Press To Passion
17. Go-Forward!
18. God's Woman of Excellence For Today: The Shunammite Woman of II Kings
19. Hannah
20. It's A Wrap!
21. Kingdom Quest I
22. Make Your Valley Full of Ditches
23. Rebuilding the Economy of the Global Kingdom of God

Printed in the United States
By Bookmasters